# WINDOWS 10 FOR SENIORS 2022

**Complete Step By Step Guide For Beginners On How To Use And Master Microsoft Windows 10 Like A Pro With Tips & Tricks**

# Nathan Jaime

**Copyright and Disclaimer:** All rights reserved. No part of this book may be reproduced without the author's permission except otherwise.

All information in this book is believed to be true and accurate as of the publication date. Neither the author nor the publisher is liable for any error or misstatement that may be made. The publisher makes no warranty, express or implied, concerning the material contained within.

©2022 by Nathan Jaime

**Publication Note:** This user guide was first published by Nathan Jaime on **August 25, 2021** and republished **March 2022** after making several improvements. This contain improved knowledge with all errors corrected and proofread for readers' best reading experience.

# Table of Contents

Introduction..............................................................8

Chapter 1: Getting Started with Windows 10 ............................11

Downloading and Installation of Windows 10 on Your Computer ............................................................................11

System Prerequisites for a Successful Installation of Windows 10 ................................................................................11

How to Set Up Your Installation Files....................................13

Installing the Files.................................................................16

Chapter 2: Navigation of Start Menu and Settings with Extensive Beginner's Overview..............................................................18

Start Menu: The Left Side.....................................................19

Start Menu: The Right Side ..................................................23

Settings.................................................................................25

**Access the Settings App** ....................................................26

**Categories Found in the Settings Application** ..................29

Chapter 3: Classic Applications in Windows 10 ......................32

How to Navigate And Use Applications ................................32

**Windows Media Player** .....................................................32

**Classic Control Panel** ........................................................33

**Internet Explorer** ..............................................................33

**Windows 10 for Solitaire Games** .....................................34

**3** | P a g e

**Windows Paint** ................................................................34

**Windows Photo Viewer** .................................................34

Chapter 4: Accessing The Windows/Microsoft Store...............36

Setting up, Sign in, Create a local Account & Sign in, Adding an Account, Switching Microsoft Accounts .........................36

**How to Set Up An Account**..............................................36

**How to Sign in**................................................................38

**Creating a Local Account** ...............................................39

**How to Add New/User and Switching Accounts**..............43

Chapter 5: Customizing Taskbar (Icon, Size, Moving, Creating folder and Apps position)............................................................44

TaskBar Navigation Setting ...................................................44

**How to Pin Apps to the Taskbar** .....................................44

**How to Move the Taskbar**...............................................45

**How to Move Icons on the Taskbar** ................................46

**How to Turn System Icons on or off and Application Icons** ................................................................................46

**How to Resize Taskbar** ...................................................47

**How to Adjust Icon Size**.................................................48

**How to Change Taskbar Colour**......................................48

**How to Open Folders in Taskbar**....................................48

**How to Hide Taskbar** ......................................................49

Chapter 6: Understanding And Mastering the Windows 10 Tray ................................................................................................50

Navigation of the Windows 10 Tray..........................................50

**How to Show Hidden Icons in the Windows 10 System Tray** .................................................................................51

**How to Show Hidden Icons in the System Tray Using the Mouse** ..............................................................................51

**How to Show Hidden Icons Using Windows 10 Settings** .52

Chapter 7: Familiarizing And Mastering Windows 10 Desktop 55

Taking a Close Insight of Windows 10 Desktop .....................55

Getting to the Desktop ...........................................................56

**How to Display/Show Desktop Icons**................................58

**How to Set Up Multiple Desktops** ...................................59

**How to Switch Between Desktops**....................................59

**How to Move Windows Between Desktops**......................60

**How to Close a Desktop** ..................................................62

Chapter 8: Maintenance, Diagnostics, and Repair.....................63

How to Update Windows and Software..................................63

How to Run Windows 10 Automatic Maintenance Feature ..64

How to Erase Unnecessary Files and Programs......................65

How to Perform Windows Maintenance Scans .....................66

Diagnostics.............................................................................66

How to Generate a Windows 10 System Diagnostic Report .67

5 | P a g e

Repair...................................................................................68

**How to Use Windows Startup Repair**...............................69

Chapter 9: Private Computer Security And Safety Tips (Security of PC)....................................................................................75

Computer Security .................................................................75

**Types of Computer Security**............................................75

**Components of Computer System**...................................76

**The CIA Triad** ...................................................................77

**Computer Security Threats** .............................................78

Why is Computer Security Important? ...............................81

Chapter 10: How to Protect Private Computer Against Installing Virus, Bugs, Unwanted Programs, and Hardware .....................82

Chapter 11: How to Setup a Remote Connection to your Computer ................................................................................87

How Does Remote Access Function?...................................87

How to Set Up Microsoft Remote Desktop Connection........88

Using the Remote Desktop App for Windows 10..................92

Chapter 12: Backing Up Your Data (External Drive & OneDrive) ..............................................................................95

External Hard Drives ............................................................95

Backing Up Your Files Online Using OneDrive ...................96

**6** | P a g e

How to Restore Your Windows 10 to its Previous State
(Factory Setting) ...................................................................98

# Introduction

**W**indows 10 serve as the most popular version of the Microsoft operating system. There have been various renditions of Windows since time past, and these include Windows 11 released October 2021, Windows 8, which was released in 2012, Windows 7 released in 2009, Windows Vista in 2006, and Windows XP in 2001. While seasoned adaptations of Windows principally ran on desktop formats and laptops, the Windows 10 is likewise intended to run similarly, well on tablets.

Looking at Windows 10, you'll observe some similarities to versions released earlier on, but you can't take away the fact that it includes many new features, elements, and enhancements. Microsoft accomplished something rather splendid with this new operating system. The split personality of Windows 8 was completely dealt with. However, the touch-friendly features were retained. Of course, everyone is delving into touch screen technology. If you've been a user of computers and Microsoft Windows versions, you'll get to observe that Windows 10 is Windows 7 with a couple of new elements and more excellent typography.

Windows 10 gets new expands on a continuous premise, accessible at no extra expense for you as a user. From Microsoft's view, it isn't a version of Windows, but it is constantly improved, more like a living software. The period where service packs, yearly pieces of updates with large sizes, and file patches existed is already over. Bugs get targeted and given the required fix, with features enhanced with software already preprogrammed.

The most recent version released, the Windows 10 May 2021 Update (known as 21H1), is generally an update required for servicing, with no new features added. The update of October 2020 (20H2) released in the past, which is not quite significant, highlighted a slicker Start menu, a more utilitarian Edge internet browser, and other beneficial changes. Windows 10 has gained much from the recent updates made in-between, for example, the News and Interests taskbar board and the Meet Now symbol seen in the Taskbar for making video conferences.

The Windows 10, with its recent updates, offers a more vigorous, more remarkable, and novel experience of computing across a scope of gadgets. An encounter streamlined for every gadget type, yet seemingly pleasant to all.

Microsoft announced on 24 June that a new version of Windows would be released. Windows 11 was released in October 2021. The new Windows form will highlight an upgraded taskbar with a unique design, **Start Menu**, and notification center alongside Teams integration, adjusted window corners with round outlook, and a Widgets feature. As a surprise, it can likewise run Android applications!

However, there is a lot to be learned from Windows 10 being the most popular version, this user guide is aimed at teaching first-timers, beginners, and seniors how to use Windows 10 efficiently and mastering the key features at a go.

# Chapter 1: Getting Started with Windows 10

## Downloading and Installation of Windows 10 on Your Computer

Without any advancement in technology, we would still find ourselves using CDs or DVDs to install Windows. Then, one has to input the files into the mediums. Nowadays, installation involves a simple process. Regardless of whether you're installing Windows 10 on a new machine or hoping to begin once again by reinstalling it on an old version, it's never been simpler to get. To do this, you'll need a USB flash drive and access to an internet connection with another computer.

### System Prerequisites for a Successful Installation of Windows 10

Install Windows 10 on your device; the requirements are pretty basic and relaxed. You don't need to bother whether your computer has a high storage capacity to run the program. Here are the base system necessities you'll require:

- Processor: 1 GHz or quicker CPU.

- RAM (Random Access Memory): At least 1 GB for the 32-bit variant of Windows 10. Or, on the other hand, 2 GB for the 64-bit version.

- Storage capacity: 16 GB or more free space on your hard drive for the 32-bit adaptation of Windows 10. You'll require 20 GB or more for 64-bit Windows 10.

- Graphic chipset: It should be viable with DirectX 9 or later, with WDDM 1.0 drivers.

- Display: It should be able to support at least 800x600 pixels.

- Internet access: Well, this might not be needed for the arrangement. In some uncommon cases (outstandingly, Windows 10 in S mode), your PC needs access to the web using Ethernet or Wi-Fi.

There should be a computer that is internet access enabled and already connected, with its setup in place for the Windows installation files. When done, get it closer to where the Windows will be installed.

**How to Set Up Your Installation Files**

- To start, get your USB drive of 8GB or more. Insert it into the drive space. A drive containing some contents will be no hindrance, but it will be wiped off during installation. A blank USB will be advisable.

- Open the Windows 10 download site with your web browser. Scroll down to the option, "Create

Windows 10 Installation Media". Tap on the "Download tool now."

- After download completion, get it running and the license agreement accepted.

- On the page indicating "What do you want to do," you'll see an option, "Create installation media for another computer." Click on it, followed by clicking on "Next," except re-installation will be done on the same computer.

- On the following page, you can tweak the installation settings for Windows 10. If the default settings aren't appealing to you, clear the checkbox for "Use the suggested alternatives for this computer" and pick the language, version, and architecture you need afterward. Click on "Next" when done.

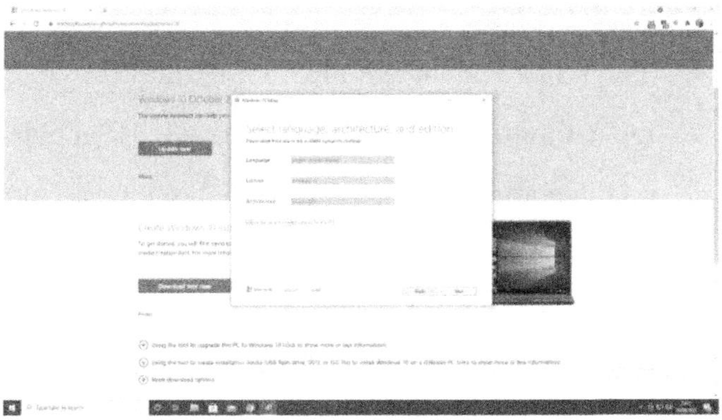

- Then, a page stating "Choose which media to use" is displayed; pick the option to burn the file into a USB flash drive. Click on "Next"

- Windows will pick up the USB drive automatically and select it. If you have more than one inserted into the drive, pick the right one, and click "Next."

- The files are then copied to the flash drive. It will take some time. When it's set, please take out the flash drive and place it into the port of the new computer requiring a fresh installation of Windows 10.

**Installing the Files**

- You'll have to change the boot request. It will enable the computer to recognize the new USB in place. Put on the computer and get to launch the UEFI or BIOS controls. It is usually done by tapping on the F1, F2, Escape or Delete key as it begins.

- When the startup menu shows up, seek out the "boot" control menu and ensure it is designed to boot from USB. Go to save the UEFI (Unified Extensible Firmware Interface)/BIOS (Basic Input/output System), and exit.

- On the computer restarting, booting should be from the USB drive. Your system will then kick off the installation program automatically. Follow up with the necessary instructions to get Windows installed on your computer.

- A license key is needed to get the Windows 10 setup completed. However, you don't require it to get Windows ready for action.

If you do not have a key at the moment, you can defer entering the key until installation is complete.

# Chapter 2: Navigation of Start Menu and Settings with Extensive Beginner's Overview

The **Start Menu** is quite an essential feature of Microsoft Windows. On opening, it brings out pieces of software that are very useful in the form of a list. These include programs, commands, and files. The activities carried out with your computer will start using the Start menu.

In Windows 10, as you've presumably seen, "Start" as a word doesn't show up on the Start menu, as it was throughout recent years; the Start menu now comes as a square button, located at the corner of the screen, on the left, showcasing the Windows logo. The name, however, is still the Start menu, and it's as yet the doorway to virtually everything on the computer.

The Start menu is parted into two segments. The left and right sides/columns.

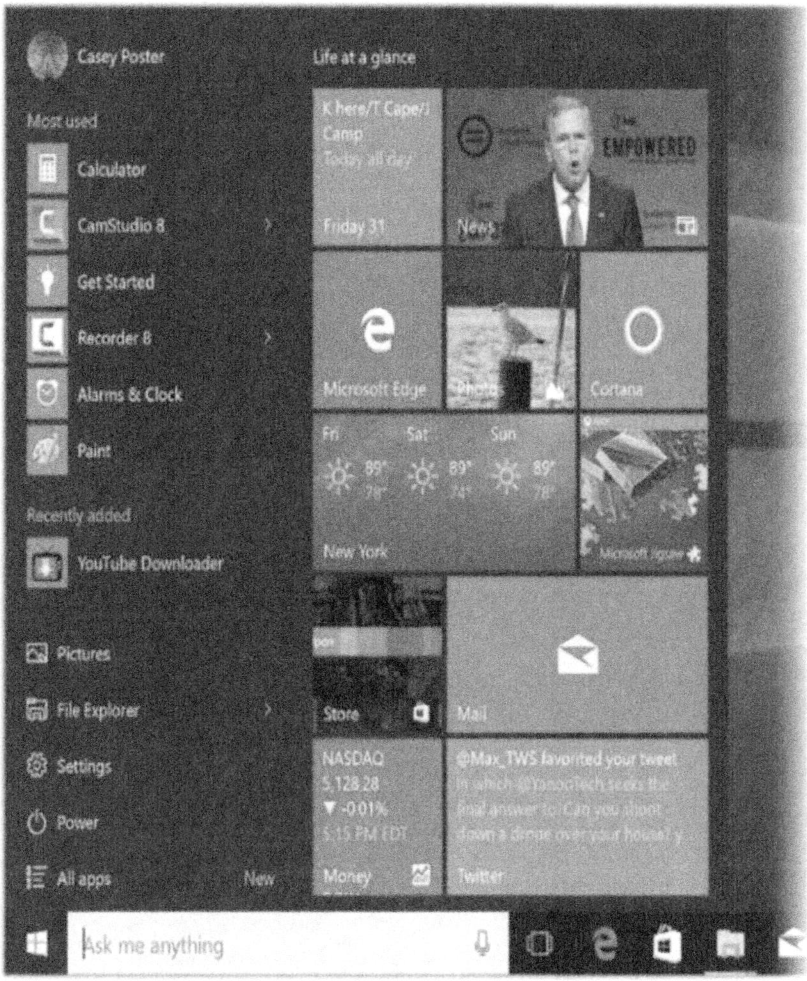

## Start Menu: The Left Side

The left partition, or something of that nature, has been a feature of Windows all along. In Windows 10, you can't get to list out all your important files, programs, and folders.

This can only be done on the right side. That left is intended to be overseen and run totally by Windows itself.

There are five sections on the left, outlined from top to bottom:

- **[Your name]**
  You get to see your account's name, including your picture at the top left corner of the menu. The image is likewise a pop-up box, giving instructions on switching using different accounts.

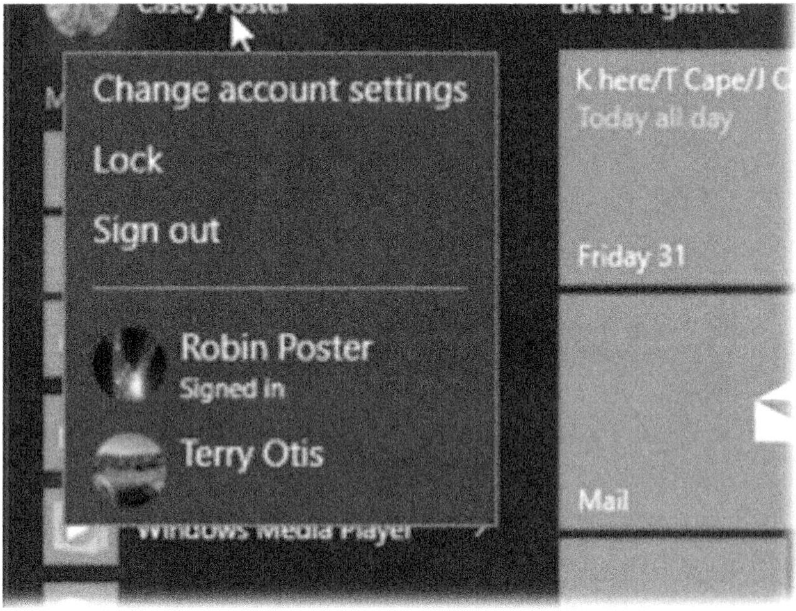

- **Most Used**

Underneath your name symbol, you get a rundown of the programs you make use of more often, as observed by Windows. This list is computed by Windows automatically and in a continuous manner. On watching a submenu arrow (>) close to a program's name in the Start menu, that's it.

- **Recently Added**

The center part of the left side shows one thing: whatever application you've downloaded or installed recently. It's shockingly helpful, particularly for beginners, who regularly get something downloaded from the net and afterward can't discover where it is.

- **Important Places**

As a general rule, the lower part of the left side is committed to posting significant spots on the computer. On a gleaming new PC, the rundown incorporates these: file explorer, all applications, settings, power.

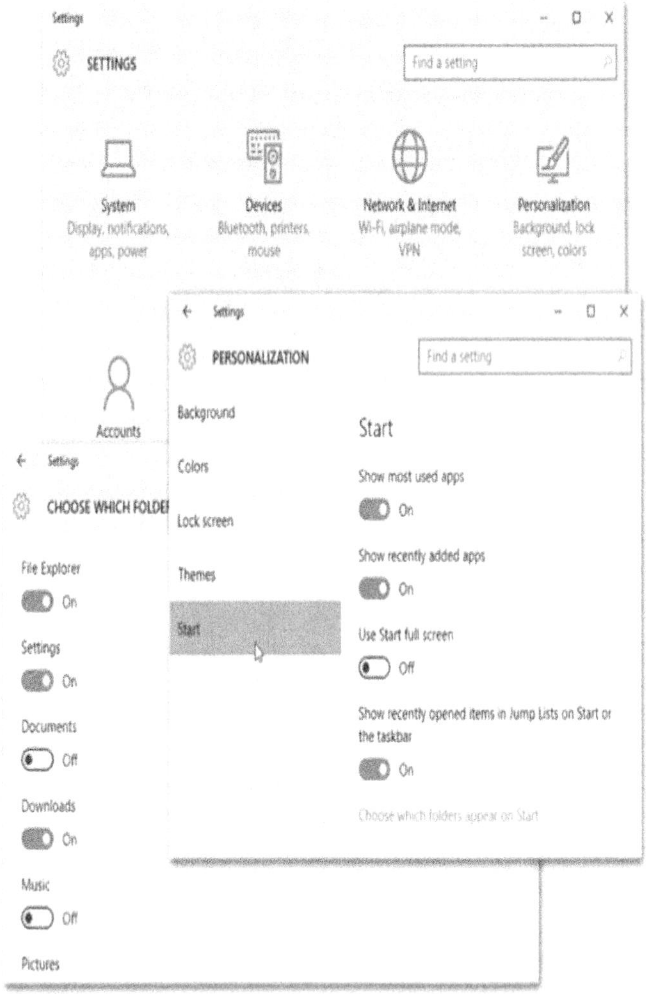

- **All Apps**

  When you click "All applications" at the lower part
  of the Start menu, what is displayed is a significant
  list undoubtedly: the expert index of each program

on your PC. You can bounce straightforwardly to your word processor, calendar/schedule, or most loved game, for instance, just by picking its name in the outlined list.

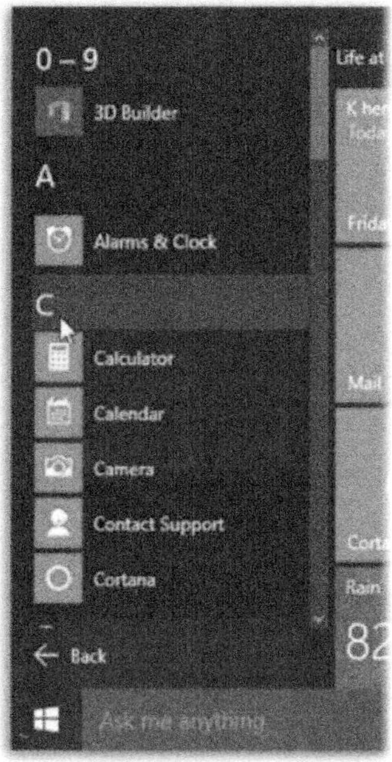

## Start Menu: The Right Side

The right half of the Start menu is the outcome of all left off the Great Touchscreen Experiment of 2012. There was an expected turnover of every computer during this period towards using a touchscreen or coming with one. A Start screen was showcased rather than a Start menu, extending from one edge to another of your screen, showing your files, folders, and other programs in the form of large rectangular tiles. There were some decent parts of the Start-screen idea, however. For an aspect, it's something beyond a launcher. It's likewise a dashboard. So in Windows 10, Microsoft chose to hold those vivid live tiles—located on the right half of the Start menu

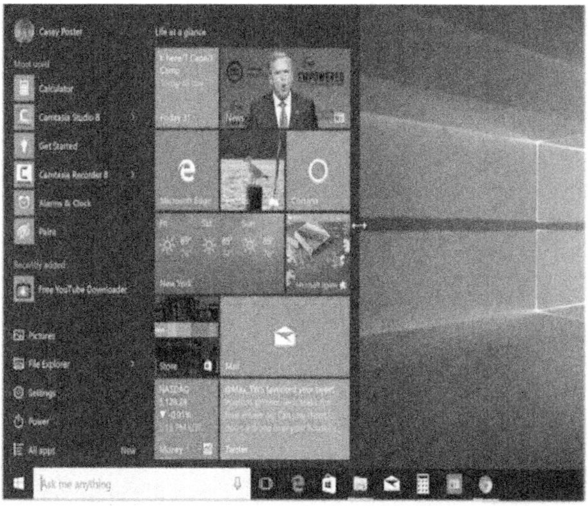

## Settings

Settings or Windows Settings is a segment of Microsoft Windows presented in Windows 8. Settings allow the user

25 | P a g e

to customize and make configurations on the operating system. Windows 10 is now referred to as "Settings," renaming it from the current "Control Panel" and replacing it. It gives access to the fundamental setup choices and settings for a client's PC. Previously, most options exclusive to the Control panel are now seen in Settings.

**Access the Settings App**
Windows 10 redesigned a great deal of the system settings into another Settings application.

- To gain access to "Settings," tap on the Start button. Or then again, Press Windows key + I to open the Settings application.

- You'll see the "Settings" option. Click on it.

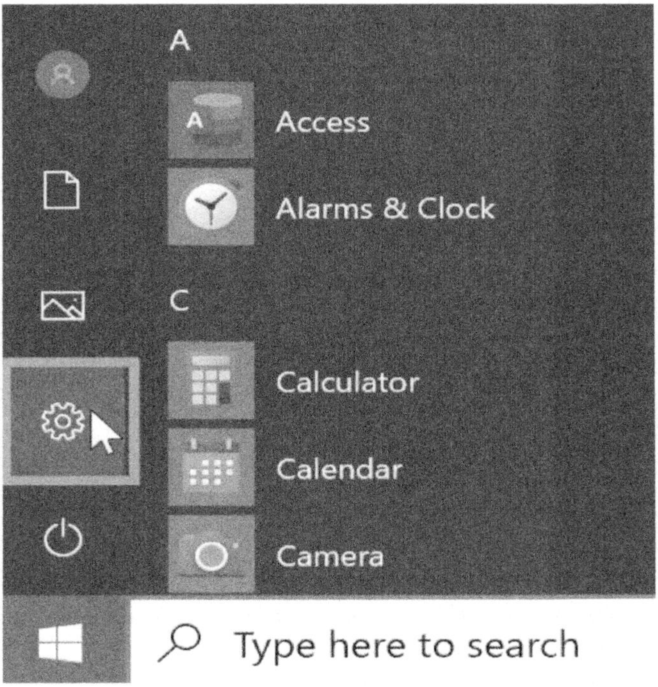

- In the Settings application, various categories envelop a large portion of your PC's settings.

Windows Settings

Find a setting

System
Display, notifications, apps, power

Devices
Bluetooth, printers, mouse

Network & Internet
Wi-Fi, airplane mode, VPN

Personalization
Background, lock screen, colors

Accounts
Your accounts, email, sync, work, family

Time & language
Speech, region, date

Ease of Access
Narrator, magnifier, high contrast

Privacy
Location, camera

- Click on a particular category to see subcategories.

- Every classification has some subcategories listed on the navigation area to the left. Click on a particular subcategory, like Notifications and activities, to see it.

- Pick a sub-class.

- Get settings customized as wanted.

- Select the gear icon to return to the primary settings page.

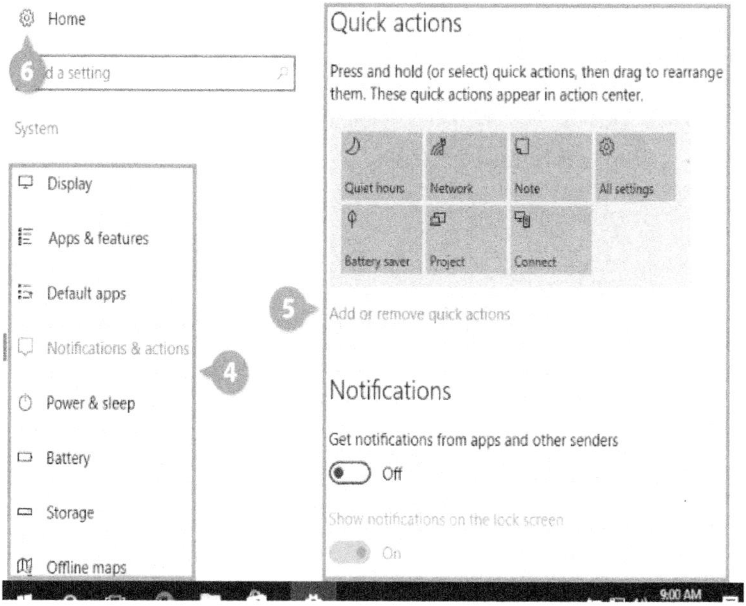

## Categories Found in the Settings Application

- System: This contains settings for your computer display, notification, app, and power.

- Devices: Contains hardware and gadgets, including Bluetooth, associated with your PC.

- Phone: This is a new Windows 10 from Fall Creators Update.

- Network and Internet: Includes settings for the network.

- Personalization allows you to change the foundation, lock screen picture, and color.

- Apps: This is a new update in Windows 10 Creators.

- Accounts: Shows associated account data and sign-in alternatives.

- Time and Language: Shows time, date, language, and local settings.

- Gaming: This was introduced in Windows 10 Anniversary Update.

- Ease of Access: This is for individuals with special needs, providing features of accessibility.

- Search

- Cortana: Thus feature was presented in Windows 10 Fall Creators Update. The latest Update, Windows 10 May 2020, has been removed.
- Privacy: This lets you figure out which applications can access your data and hardware.

- Update and Security: This is a setting for Windows updates and security.

# Chapter 3: Classic Applications in Windows 10

## How to Navigate And Use Applications

Microsoft keeps on devising several means to modernize Windows 10. Each new update brings with it cool new features. In any case, other classic Windows applications you've been utilizing for quite a long time while not given any necessary promotions are still being seen. Here are some traditional applications:

### Windows Media Player

If you want to watch videos using Windows 10, there is a new introduction to advanced Movies and TV applications. Also, you might have seen that the music player is Groove Music, as a default even though it put an end to the streaming service of Groove Music Pass for Spotify.

Microsoft Groove is the default present-day music application to push play to files containing your local music and tunes saved to OneDrive.

Well, the Windows Media Player is still very much available if you're changing over from version 7 to 10 or if you've been a regular user of the media player. To locate the Windows

Media Player, tap the Windows key and input "wmp" or the Cortana search box.

## Classic Control Panel

You may very well be inclined to find system settings using the classic method instead of searching through the Settings app. It is possible to get to Control Panel. However, it merits becoming accustomed to the new Settings application as Control Panel will not be around for long, and the Settings application keeps on improving.

In previous adaptations of Windows 10, locating the Control Panel is done using the "power user menu." Get access by right-clicking the Start symbol. However, even that has been taken out. Thus, to locate it, tap on the Windows key and type: "control panel" or "CPL" to get to it.

## Internet Explorer

For Windows 10, the new default is the Microsoft Edge. If you require or incline toward Internet Explorer, tap on the Windows button and input "Internet Explorer" or "IE" 11 or make use of the search box, and it will show up at the top under best matches. If you utilize IE a great deal, you can stick it to your Start menu or Taskbar by right-clicking it after searching.

**Windows 10 for Solitaire Games**

Klondike Solitaire was one of the exceptional games seen. The gameplay was quite simple and fulfilling. But keep in mind that Windows 10 does accompany the Microsoft Solitaire collection, which includes the classic Klondike Solitaire. This version is relatively new, with slicker features and decks that can be solvable. You can get the definitive version of this game for free on three Windows stores.

**Windows Paint**

Microsoft Paint is still available. It may not be seen on your Windows 10 PC except if you get to download it yourself. The Paint 3D application has replaced Microsoft Paint. However, after an immense objection from committed fans, Microsoft has vowed to make it accessible in the Microsoft Store.

**Windows Photo Viewer**

Windows Photo Viewer is a no-muddle, straightforward, pretty basic, and easy approach to view pictures. The Photos app has replaced this Photo Viewer, which has good editing features. However, Windows Photo Viewer is excellent if you need a simple method to see photographs without entirely different elements. It has an essential one-touch slideshow work and print and Email photos options.

Changing the computer's registry is necessary to download and install the files.

# Chapter 4: Accessing The Windows/Microsoft Store

## Setting up, Sign in, Create a local Account & Sign in, Adding an Account, Switching Microsoft Accounts

The Microsoft Store, known beforehand as Windows Store, is a platform for distributing digital products claimed by Microsoft. Universal apps, game consoles, and digital video are distributed under the Windows platform.

### How to Set Up An Account

You can access the contents of the Microsoft Store using only one login. A username and password connect you to all the contents from the Store, Office, to Skype, Xbox, and others.

- Go to the Windows Account page for Microsoft and click on "Create a free Microsoft account."

## One account for all things Microsoft

When you set up your Microsoft account across your devices and services, the things that matter most to you – like people, documents, photos, and settings – follow you on whatever devices you're using. Your Microsoft account lets you flow freely from task to task and make the most of every moment. It not only gives you access to Microsoft services, but also makes them work together in a way that's all about you.

Sign in

Create a free Microsoft account

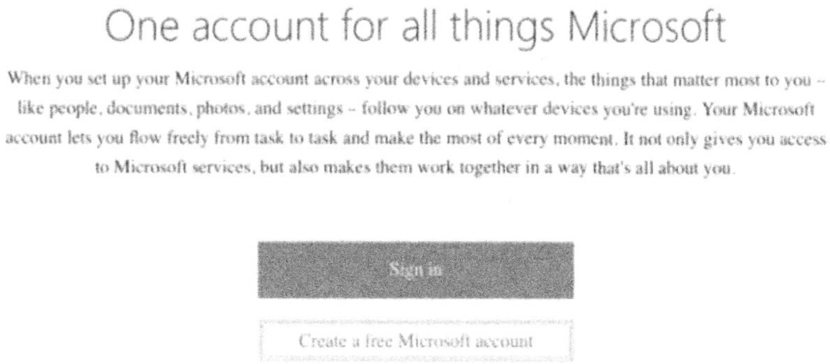

- Input the required information and create a password. We are setting up a new email account on a personal account different from the Microsoft account.
- A Captcha code is seen. Input the code.

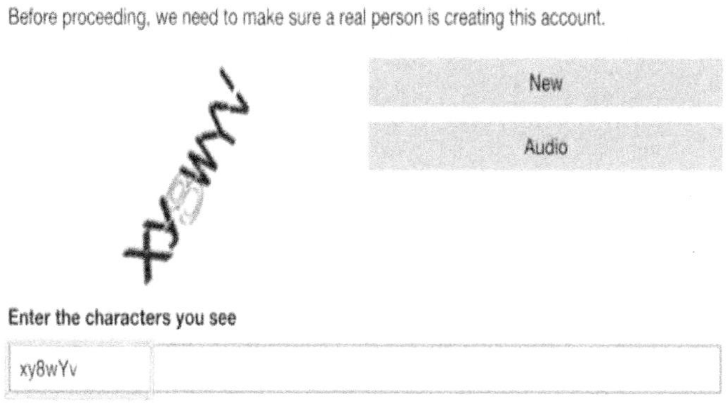

Before proceeding, we need to make sure a real person is creating this account.

New

Audio

**Enter the characters you see**

xy8wYv

- Select "Create an account."

Send me promotional offers from Microsoft. You can unsubscribe at any time.

Click **Create account** to agree to the Microsoft Services Agreement and privacy and cookies statement.

Create account

- Verification of your email account is next.

Verify your email address  Inbox  x

**Microsoft account team** <account-security-noreply@account.microsoft.com>
to me

Microsoft account

# Verify your email address

To finish setting up this Microsoft account, we just need to make sure this email address is yours.

Verify afak33mailaddr3ss@gmail.com

**How to Sign in**

- Proceed to your Microsoft account and click on "Sign in."

- Input the correct email address, phone number, or Skype details used for other services. Click on "Next." On account of not having a Microsoft account, select "No account? Create one."

- Add your password.

- Click on "Sign in."

## Creating a Local Account

- Get to the "Settings" page or press Win+1 using your keyword. Click on "Account."

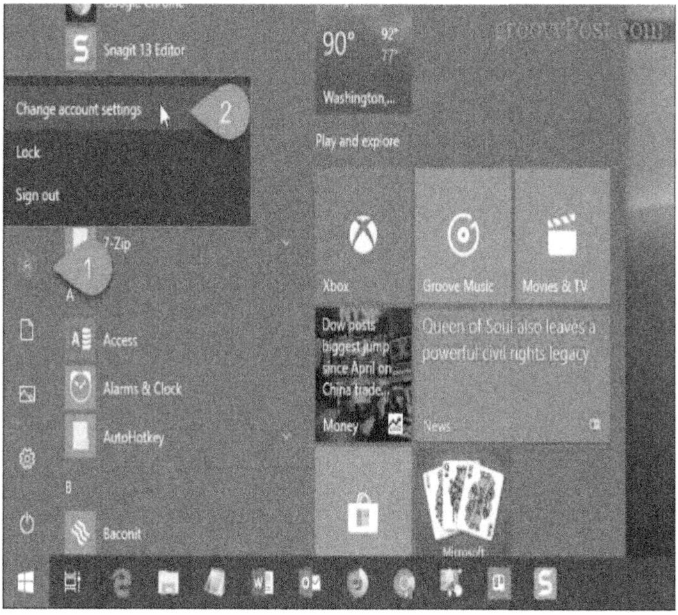

- From the Account settings, click on "Family & other users" seen on the left column. Check the right side and click the "+" button, which is by the side of "Add someone else."

- There's a prompt to add the Microsoft account's Email or number. Click on the option station. You don't have the sign-in information, seen underneath.

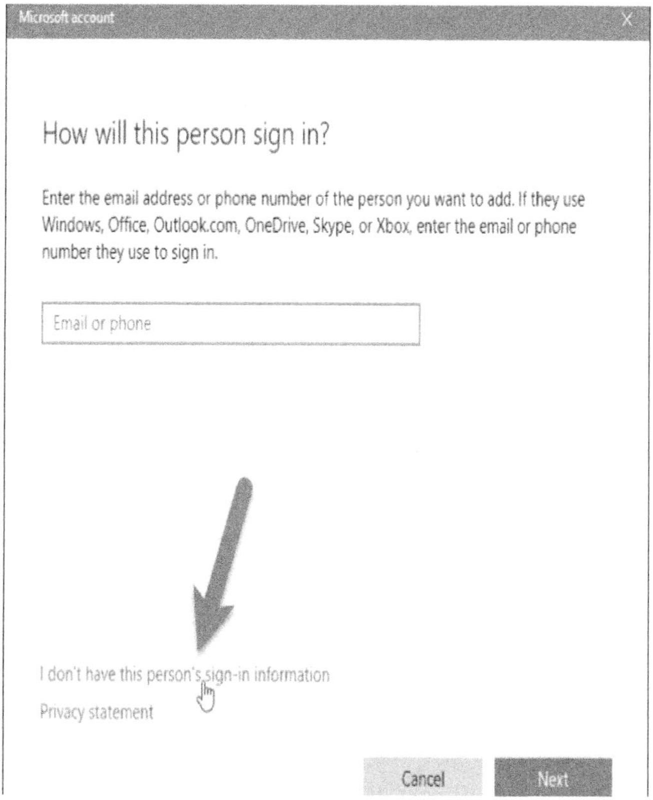

- You'll be urged to create an account. Click on "Add a user without a Microsoft account." Select " Next. "

## Let's create your account

Windows, Office, Outlook.com, OneDrive, Skype, Xbox. They're all better and more personal when you sign in with your Microsoft account.* Learn more

someone@example.com

Get a new email address

Password

United States

Birth month | Day | Year

*If you already use a Microsoft service, go Back to sign in with that account.

Add a user without a Microsoft account

Back    Next

- Put in the name you want. Add a password and ensure the account is verified.

- There are about six fields at the bottom to help recover your password if you forget.

- Complete three of the security questions and select" Next."

- An account is now created.

## How to Add New/User and Switching Accounts

- Go to" Settings."

- Click on" Accounts."

- Proceed to" Email and accounts."

- The" Add a Microsoft account" is selected.

- Input the details of your personal Microsoft account. Save and then proceed to the Microsoft Store app.

- When in Microsoft Store, click on "Sign in." You'll see the Microsoft account newly added. Select it.

- If another account is already signed in, sign out and log in back into the Store using the new Microsoft account.

# Chapter 5: Customizing Taskbar (Icon, Size, Moving, Creating folder and Apps position)

## TaskBar Navigation Setting

The Windows 10 taskbar works similarly to past Windows forms, offering alternate routes and symbols for each running application. Windows 10 provides a wide range of approaches to modify the Taskbar as you would prefer. With a tiny bit of work, you can change the Taskbar to make it run in the way you like.

### How to Pin Apps to the Taskbar

Pinning apps can be done from the Start menu or the Start screen and the Apps list. Go to the Start menu, click on it, then right-click on any application symbol or tile. Click on "More," then "Pin to taskbar." Pinning locks the app to the Taskbar. If you want to remove it, move to the icon for the Taskbar, right-click on it and select Unpin from Taskbar.

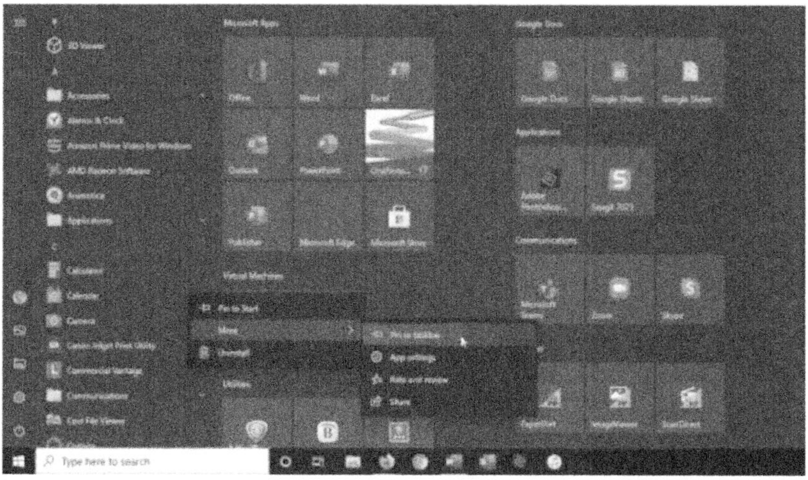

## How to Move the Taskbar

The original position of the Taskbar is set to base, and you can bring a change to its place, either to the top, left, or to the right.

To get the position changed from the bottom to the top, move over to "Settings," click on it and look for "Personalization," then "Taskbar." Select "top" from the "Taskbar position on the screen" option.

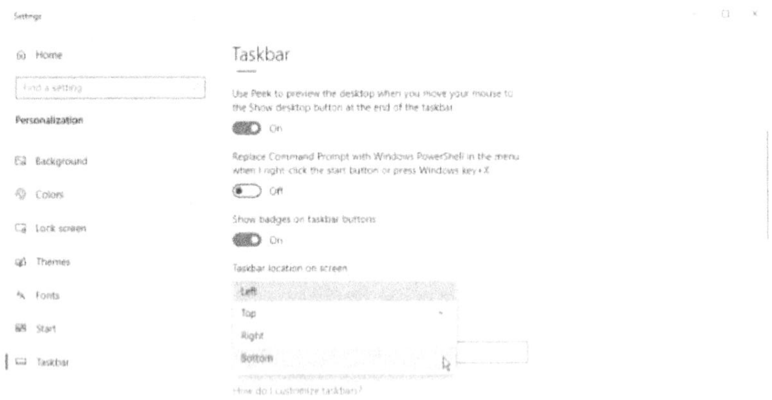

## How to Move Icons on the Taskbar

If you aren't appeased with the positioning of icons seen on the Taskbar, you can still move them. Push down on an icon using your mouse or with your finger if you're making use of a touchscreen device. Move the held-down icon to your preferred position, either right or left.

Drag it to one side or right with your mouse (or finger on a touchscreen gadget). Let go of the icon when it is now in your new favored spot.

## How to Turn System Icons on or off and Application Icons

All system icons are observed to be placed at the right of the Taskbar, to the extreme. These icons can be turned off or on. To turn it off, click on "Settings," then "Personalization," go-to "Taskbar," and tap on the "Turn system icons on or off," and this can be located beneath the Notification area section. Once in the Window, the icons you don't need can then be turned off.

## How to Resize Taskbar

Suppose you have countless such icons settled on the Taskbar that there's scarcely space for them on a solitary row. Resize the Taskbar to increase the height. Get the top line of the Taskbar and drag it up until it takes up at least two rows. If you choose to dispose of the vast majority of the icons, you can lessen the height of the Taskbar back to a row by hauling down the border at the top.

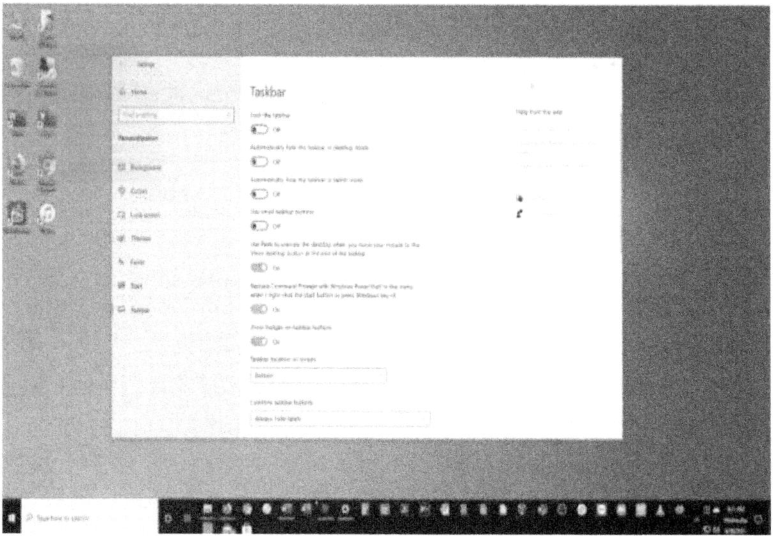

## How to Adjust Icon Size

If more icons are added to the Taskbar, Open Taskbar settings and get the option "Use small Taskbar" turned on. It will make the current icons shrivel. On observation of the icons being excessively little, please return to the settings of the Taskbar and turn it off to take them to their bigger size.

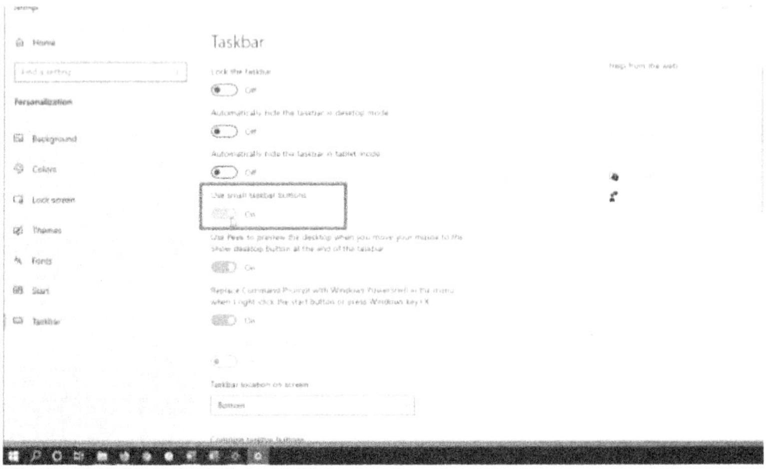

## How to Change Taskbar Colour

To change the color of the Taskbar, go to "Settings," click on "Personalization," then "Colours," and search for the option, "Show accent color on the following surfaces" and ensure the "Start, taskbar, and action center" box is checked.

## How to Open Folders in Taskbar

Opening folders gives you the option to see files content without the hassle of going through indexes. First, right-click on the space unused in the Taskbar. Click on "Toolbars" and then "New toolbar. Scroll to an index and select the "Select Folder" option is selected. You can now get to open that file straight from the Taskbar.

## How to Hide Taskbar

Suppose you need the Taskbar to stay invisible except if you move your mouse to its area. With your system in desktop mode, get to open the Taskbar settings. The option saying "Automatically hide the Taskbar" is then turned on. It should be in desktop mode.

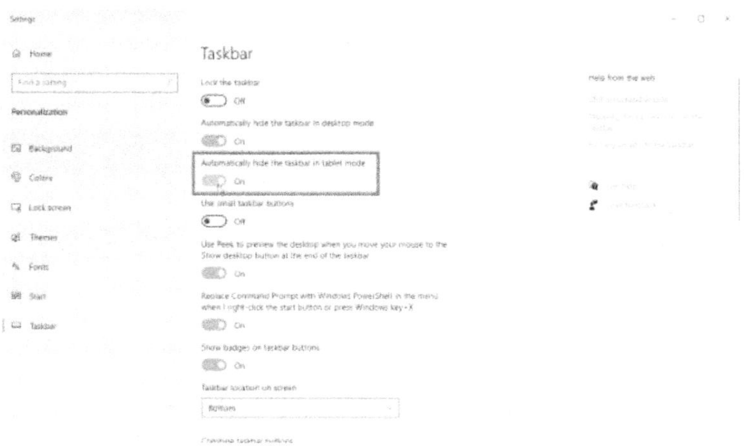

# Chapter 6: Understanding And Mastering the Windows 10 Tray

## Navigation of the Windows 10 Tray

The System Tray is also known as Notification Area. It can be seen located at the right half of the Windows Taskbar.

The System Tray highlights various sorts of notifications and also alert systems coming from your computer, like connection to the internet or the volume level, and has been recognized with Windows for more than 20 years. It continued improving since it was first presented with Windows 95, making accessibility to system functions, applications, and notifications quiet.

Windows 10 now allows simple customization, more than before. In this case, you can tweak the system applications and icons shown on it. Regardless of whether you need to conceal the volume symbol, keep a specific icon consistently noticeable in the Notification region, or see only the clock on your Taskbar,

## How to Show Hidden Icons in the Windows 10 System Tray

The Windows 10 System Tray comprises a segment of consistently visible icons and another section that can be seen when you click on the system tray in expanded format. For icons observed to be hidden in the raised tray, displaying it involves dragging it away from the expanded tray onto the standard.

## How to Show Hidden Icons in the System Tray Using the Mouse

In Windows 10, many icons are hidden on the expandable tray. By default, it gives you a good space amount on the Taskbar. While to uncover them, the arrow on the Notification region should be clicked.

The most precise approach to showing any icons in your Notification region is to drag them using the cursor from the expandable sheet instead of the Taskbar.

Drag the hidden icon to where you want to see it

A great tip is to place the settings on "Always show icons in the notification area." This option removes the arrow and expandable tray.

## How to Show Hidden Icons Using Windows 10 Settings

Another strategy for showing icons already hidden in the tray includes getting to the Taskbar settings. Doing this involves right-clicking on an unused space or just pressing and holding on to the Taskbar area. The menu is displayed. Locate Taskbar settings and click on it.

**52** | P a g e

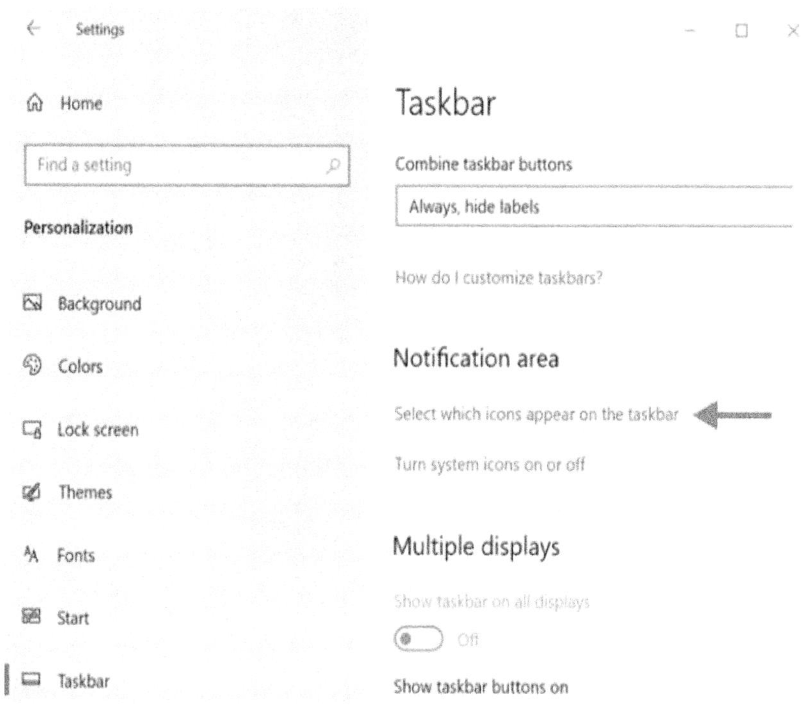

← Settings                                    —  ☐  ×

⌂ Home

Find a setting                          ⌕

Personalization

🖼 Background

🎨 Colors

🖵 Lock screen

🖌 Themes

ᴬA Fonts

🎮 Start

🖵 Taskbar

# Taskbar

Combine taskbar buttons

Always, hide labels

How do I customize taskbars?

## Notification area

Select which icons appear on the taskbar  ◄━━━━━

Turn system icons on or off

## Multiple displays

Show taskbar on all displays

⬤◯ Off

Show taskbar buttons on

From the Taskbar settings, a part of the Settings app, look down the rundown of settings seen on the right half of the Window until you discover the Notification region. The "Select which icons show up on the taskbar" option is seen.

Each of the icons you need in the Notification region is turned on. The chosen icons you decide to show become immediately apparent on the Taskbar.

**53** | P a g e

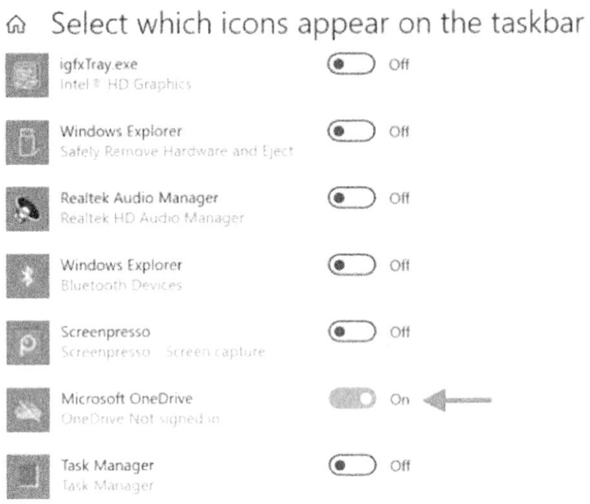

## ⌂ Select which icons appear on the taskbar

| | | |
|---|---|---|
| igfxTray.exe | ⬤ ) | Off |
| Intel ® HD Graphics | | |
| Windows Explorer | ⬤ ) | Off |
| Safely Remove Hardware and Eject | | |
| Realtek Audio Manager | ⬤ ) | Off |
| Realtek HD Audio Manager | | |
| Windows Explorer | ⬤ ) | Off |
| Bluetooth Devices | | |
| Screenpresso | ⬤ ) | Off |
| Screenpresso - Screen capture | | |
| Microsoft OneDrive | ( ⬤ | On ← |
| OneDrive Not signed in | | |
| Task Manager | ⬤ ) | Off |
| Task Manager | | |

Take note that if a switch is turned on to show a specific icon and that icon isn't immediately displayed on your Taskbar, the application may be most likely not running on your PC. Remember that the icons in your Notification region are possibly displayed when they are running in the background.

If you like to watch out for everything, you can utilize the option of "Always show all icons in the notification area" seen at the top list. Toggle on the switch close to it, and every one of the icons in the rundown is immediately shown in your Taskbar, while their settings, presently old, can't be given changes.

**54** | P a g e

# Chapter 7: Familiarizing And Mastering Windows 10 Desktop

## Taking a Close Insight of Windows 10 Desktop

The Windows 10 desktop allows you to run a few applications and programs simultaneously, and each runs inside its little Window. That detachment enables you to spread a few programs over the screen and bits of information shared among all.

At first installation, the Window area is seen as anew, almost blank Desktop displayed. After getting to work on some tasks and projects, the number of icons on the Desktop will increase. Loading of these icons needs a quick double-click. Many individuals leave their Desktop loaded with icons for simple access. Some others put together their work: Files are stored in an organizer when they are chipping away at something.

Regardless of how you utilize the Desktop, there is mainly three fundamental part to it:

- **Start button:** To dispatch a program, tap on the Start button/menu located in the lower-left corner on the

Desktop. Once it opens, identify the app name or tile you need to run. Click on it.

- **Taskbar:** Resting apathetically along the base edge of your screen, the Taskbar shows a list of apps and programs that are currently open or running and contains icons for dispatching a couple of projects. You can see the icon's name under operation by dragging your cursor over it, together with the app's thumbnail.

- **Recycle Bin:** The Recycle Bin on the Desktop, which looks similar to a wastebasket shape, stores files recently deleted for simple recovery.

**Getting to the Desktop**

If you need to get to your Windows 10 Desktop quickly, there are a few approaches.

- Click Icon to Show the Desktop
  An icon is located in the right corner at the lower end of the screen, with a rectangle. Click on this icon. It

is also closer to the notification icon. To go back to the Windows opened before, click on the icon again.

- Use the Taskbar Menu

  Move to the Taskbar and right-click. Ensure you click on a vacant space. Select "Show the desktop" seen from the menu.

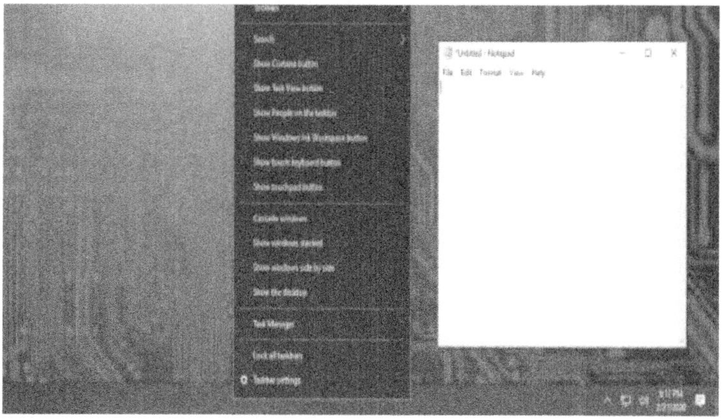

- Use a Keyboard Shortcut

  Tap on the Windows Key + D to flip to and fro from the Desktop.

## How to Display/Show Desktop Icons

The icons on your Desktop may well be hidden. To see them, right-click on the Desktop, click on "View," and then tap on "Show desktop icons." Icons such as This PC, Recycle Bin, and others can be added to the Desktop.

- Click on the "Start menu," then move to "Settings," open and select "Personalization," then "Themes."

- From "Themes," click "Related Settings" select "Desktop icon settings."

- Pick the icons to be shown on your Desktop, then click on "Apply and OK."

## How to Set Up Multiple Desktops

Windows 10 acquaints a way to set up multiple desktops on a monitor. It is known as a virtual Desktop. You can get to swap the Desktop into view, allowing you to move your work starting with one Desktop then onto the next. That can be convenient for individuals with tiny screens who need to flip among a few arrangements of adjoining windows.

The "Task View" plane is first opened to create a virtual desktop. It is done by clicking on the "Task View," seen as a rectangle on overlapping form, located on the Taskbar. You can also do this by tapping the Windows Key + Tab. After accessing the "Task View" plane, click on "New desktop" to create a virtual desktop. An alternate route in the form of a keyboard shortcut, Windows Key + Ctrl + D, can be used.

## How to Switch Between Desktops

To switch, click on the "Task View" plane and pick on the Desktop to switch to. You can also use Windows Key + Ctrl + Left Arrow and Windows Key + Ctrl + Right Arrow.

## How to Move Windows Between Desktops

- Open the "Task View" plane and afterward float over the Desktop containing the Window to be moved. The Windows on that Desktop will spring up.

- Look out for the Windows to be moved, then right-click, select "Move to," and pick the Desktop you need to move the Window to. The drag and drop option can also be used.

- Pick the Windows that needs to be moved and drag them into the ideal Desktop.

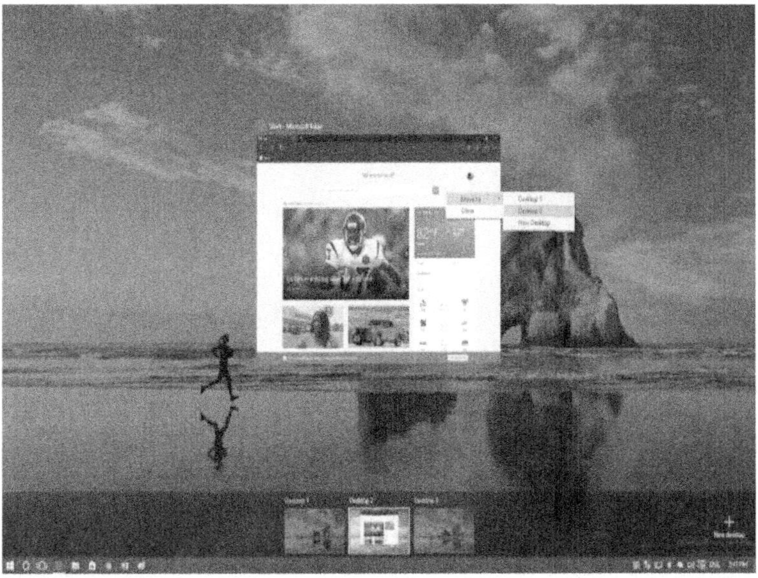

Desktop 1
Desktop 2
Desktop 3
New desktop

**How to Close a Desktop**

- Click the Task View" plane and drift over the Desktop to be closed until a little "X" is seen in the upper right corner.

- Click on the "X," and the Desktop is closed.

# Chapter 8: Maintenance, Diagnostics, and Repair

Owning a personal computer is incredible. However, you should set aside the effort to carry out some essential tasks of maintaining Windows to ensure your machine performs optimally. It's very much possible that the little time and effort not put into Maintenance can transform into long periods of extra work later on.

## How to Update Windows and Software

Being current with the latest is perhaps the most fundamental, however significant, Windows maintenance undertakings. Windows 10 is incredible about its update. However, you should always check in to ensure it's not delayed or prevented now and then. To update your Windows:

- Move to "Settings," then "Update and Security."

- Select "Windows Update" and tap "Check for Updates."

You'll be noted by Windows if there are any updates. New updates should be installed automatically. While you're chipping away at updates, it's a smart thought to ensure all your software, already installed, is updated.

## How to Run Windows 10 Automatic Maintenance Feature

The principal thing is to get the Windows 10 Automatic Maintenance to feature up and running. Automatic Maintenance has already been set to default to occur at 2:00 am, once a day, at the point when you are not making use of your computer actively, but it is switched on.

This component can perform updates on the system and apps, scans for security and malware detection, disk optimization and defragmentation, diagnostics, and other functions. To run the maintenance feature:

- Go to the Control Panel. Open "System and Security."

- Click on "Security and Maintenance" and afterward extend the Maintenance segment.

- Click "Start maintenance." It is done if your computer hasn't performed the task.

**How to Erase Unnecessary Files and Programs**

As you utilize your computer more and more, for more extended periods, there will be increasing, more junk or un-useful files on your PC so that it will run increasingly slow. Also, erasing superfluous files is not needed to maintain your computer. Also, if there are countless projects on your PC, your PC will run slow.

**How to Perform Windows Maintenance Scans**

As a feature of maintaining Windows 10, occasional scans should be done for Maintenance to ensure there isn't an issue you've neglected. You should perform an SFC Scan consistently to check whether there is any bad system file, and in case there is, the SFC device will automatically get it fixed. Here is the best approach to run it.

- Input "cmd" in the box for search, and afterward, right-click on the Command Prompt to pick "Run as administrator." Select "Yes."

- "SFC/scan now" is then inputted the Window that pops out. Tap "Enter."

- Allow the scan to complete.

**Diagnostics**

The System Diagnostic Report is a critical aspect of a performance monitor. It can show hardware and their resources, system reaction times, and computer processes, alongside information system and setup data.

## How to Generate a Windows 10 System Diagnostic Report

It would help if you were signed in as an Administrator to generate the report. Tap on the Windows Key + R with your keyboard to dispatch the "Run dialog" box and type in: "perfmon/report" and click "Enter" or "OK." You can run that equivalent order from the "Command Prompt" (Admin) to create the report, as well.

The Resource and Performance Monitor will show up, and you'll get to see the analytic test running – it requires an entire minute to finish. At the point when it completes, notwithstanding general information or summary of the system health, you'll notice superior outcomes recorded by different parts. It gives information on components like the CPU, Network, Memory, and the diagnostics of programming setups.

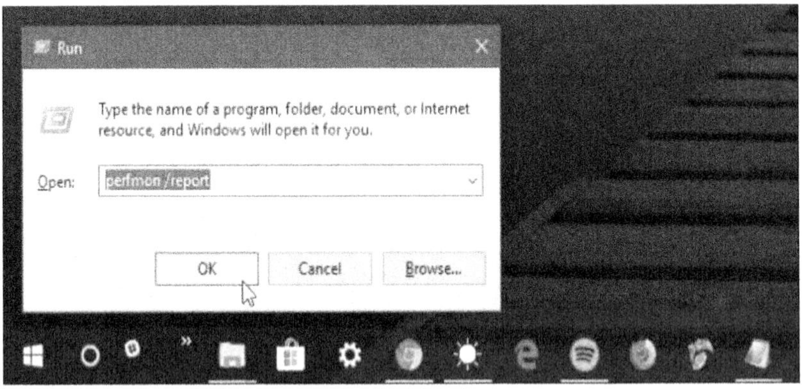

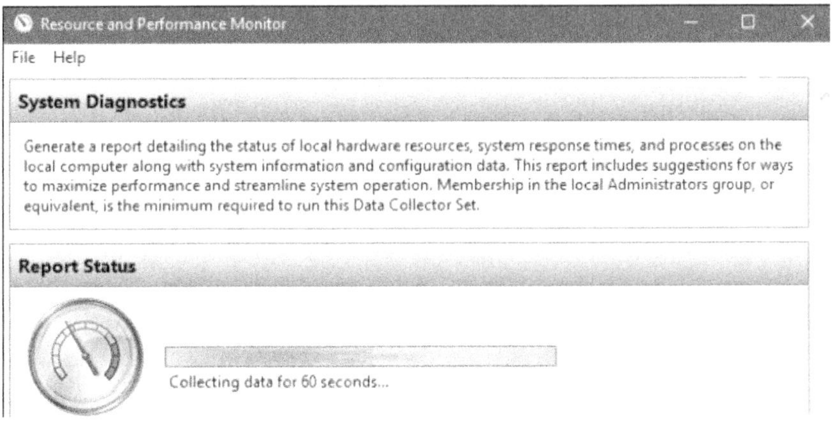

## Repair

In some cases, a Windows 10 system will start performing poorly to the required repair. At the point when your Windows 10 PC isn't functioning admirably, can't boot well, freezes, or shows black or blue or blue errors on the screen, you can take perform a few tasks to fix Windows 10 issues to return your PC once again to its normal state. Follow these methods to fix Windows 10.

### How to Use Windows Startup Repair

Windows 10 is not booting up properly and bringing up the login screen or Desktop. Your initial step ought to be to utilize Startup Repair. Here's the process:

- Go to the Windows 10 "Advanced Startup Options" menu. On numerous PCs, tapping the F11 button immediately you power on will take you directly to the Windows 10 Advanced Startup Options. Boot off the internal disk and click "Next," followed by "Repair."

When your PC has booted, select "Troubleshoot."

And afterward, you'll have to select "Advanced options."

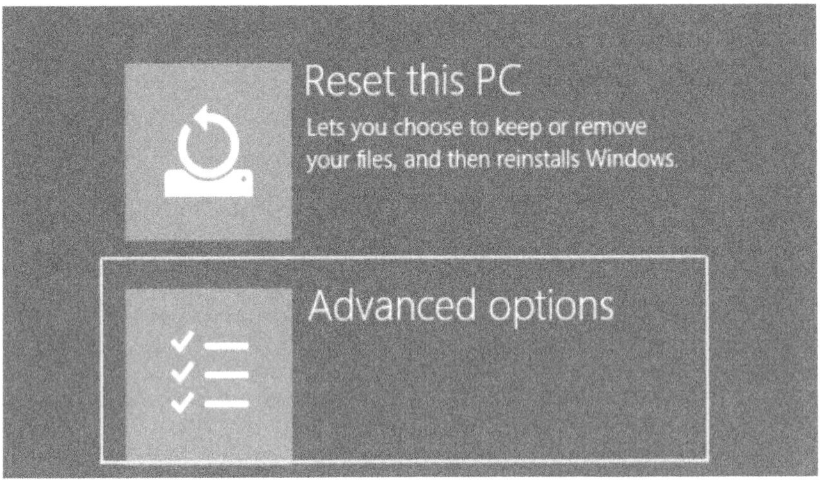

**Reset this PC**
Lets you choose to keep or remove your files, and then reinstalls Windows.

**Advanced options**

- Click Startup Repair.

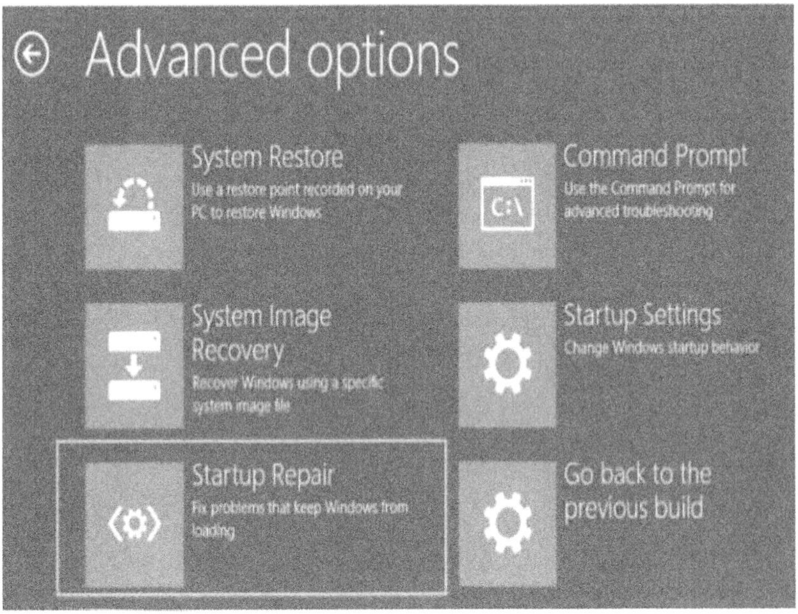

⊕ **Advanced options**

**System Restore**
Use a restore point recorded on your PC to restore Windows

**Command Prompt**
Use the Command Prompt for advanced troubleshooting

**System Image Recovery**
Recover Windows using a specific system image file

**Startup Settings**
Change Windows startup behavior

**Startup Repair**
Fix problems that keep Windows from loading

**Go back to the previous build**

Windows will take some time to fix the issue between seconds to minutes.

- Use Windows Restore

Go to the Windows 10 "Advanced Startup Options" menu using the above guide.
Select System Restore.

Allow the computer to reboot.

Select your username.

Input your password.

A restore point is to be selected from the menu. Continue with the prompts. Note that this method can't be used without a restore point.

Perform a Disk Scan

The problems surrounding your Windows 10 might originate from the wrong file. If it's possible to boot into the operating system, regardless of whether you

need to boot into protected mode, there's a need to do
a file scan to check for issues.

Input "cmd" into the search box.

You'll see a Command Prompt. Right-click on it and
"Run as Administrator."

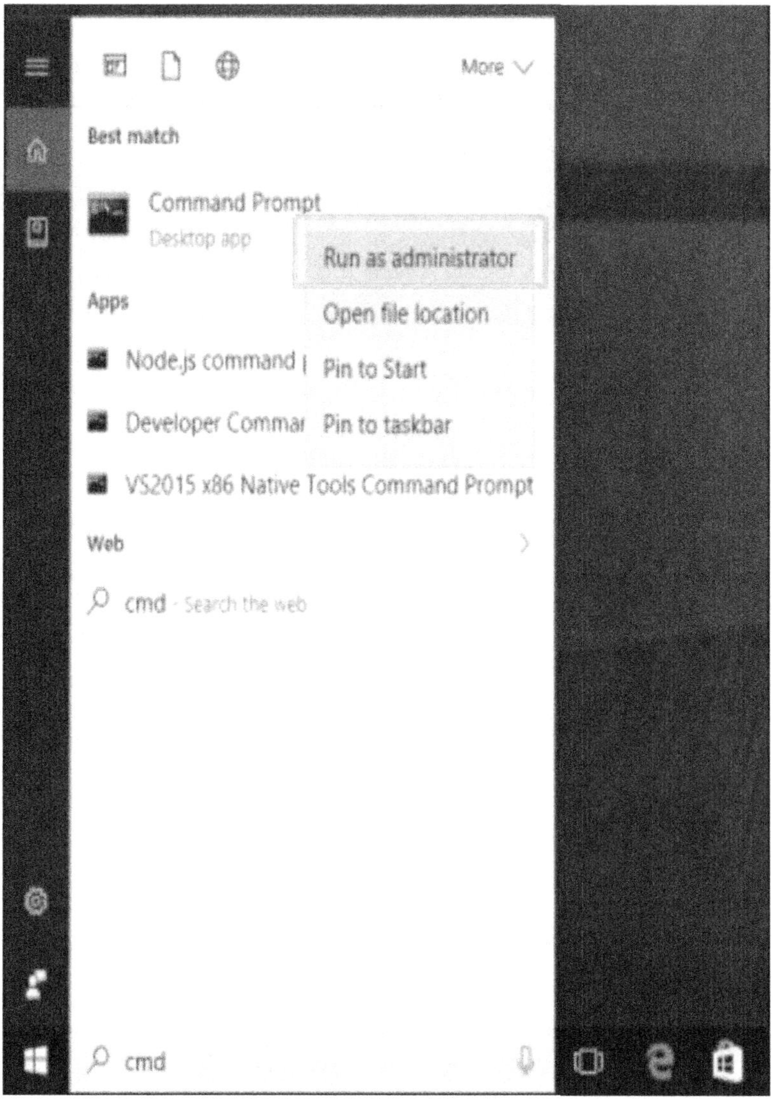

Type SFC/scan now at order brief and click "Enter."

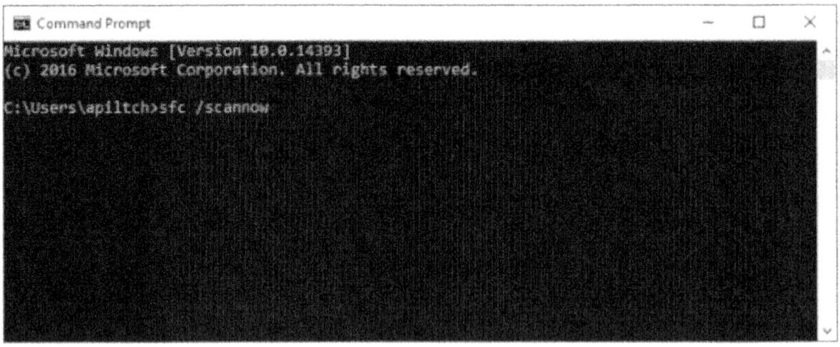

```
Command Prompt                                    —   □   ×

Microsoft Windows [Version 10.0.14393]
(c) 2016 Microsoft Corporation. All rights reserved.

C:\Users\apiltch>sfc /scannow
```

Scanning will take some time. Any ruined files it finds will be fixed.

# Chapter 9: Private Computer Security And Safety Tips (Security of PC)

## Computer Security

It refers to providing security for computers, laptops, and other devices using advanced technologies over a network. PC security usually involves computer networks of both private and public entities.

More so, the security of computers is fundamentally the provision of protection to computer systems and data from being damaged, stolen, and used inappropriately without approval. It is the most common way of forestalling and preventing unapproved utilization of your computer. PC security is fundamentally critical to forestall change or harm because of any form of malicious threats.

### Types of Computer Security

Different kinds of PC security are generally used to ensure the critical data of an organization:

- Information/data security is getting data secured from unapproved access, change, and erasure.

- Application Security is getting to secure an application by developing security components to keep them from cyber threats like an injection of SQL, DoS attacks information breach, and so on

- PC Security implies protecting an independent machine by regular updating tasks and patching.

- Network Security involves hardware and software technologies being well secured.

- Cybersecurity is characterized by offering security on computer systems with continuous interaction/association over computer networks.

**Components of Computer System**
The segments of a PC framework that should be given maximum security and protection are:

- Hardware is the actual part of a computer similar to the system memory and disk drive.

- Firmware: long-lasting programming that is carved into a hardware gadget's nonvolatile memory and is generally undetectable to the client

- Software: a programming offering services such as operating system, word processor, web browser to the client.

## The CIA Triad

PC security is mostly about three fundamental areas:

- Confidentiality

- Integrity

- Availability

Confidentiality guarantees that data is accessible just to the target group.

Integrity is shielding data/information from being changed by unapproved parties.

Availability ensures the effective running of networks, applications, and systems.

In basic language, PC security ensures that the computer's data and components are in good shape and available for use, yet secured from individuals or software that shouldn't get to it or alter it.

## Computer Security Threats

Security threats to computers are potential risks that might conceivably hamper or prevent the computer from functioning optimally. At present, threats of various types are constantly rising as the world advances.

The threats posing huge dangers to computer security are:

**Viruses**

Viruses that attack computers are malicious programs stacked into the client's PC without the client's information. It multiplies itself and taints the documents and programs on the client's PC. A definitive objective of a computer virus is to guarantee that the casualty's PC won't ever have the option to work appropriately or even by any means.

## Computer Worm

Computer worm can duplicate itself starting with one PC then onto the next, without human involvement. The common threat here is that it will occupy all spaces available in your hard disk because a worm can reproduce in large volume and with incredible speed.

## Phishing

Phishing is camouflaging as a dependable individual or business; phishers endeavor to take delicate monetary or individual's personal information using false Emails or texts. Phishing is, sadly, extremely simple to execute. You are convinced that it's the actual mail and that you might enter your data.

## Botnet

A botnet is a gathering of computers with good internet access that have been undermined by a programmer making use of a virus. A standalone computer is called a 'zombie PC.' The aftereffect of this threat is the casualty's PC. In this case, the bot will be utilized for malignant exercises and a more powerful attack like DDoS.

**Rootkit**

A rootkit is a PC program intended to give unrestricted access while effectively concealing its presence. On installation of a Rootkit, the regulator of the rootkit will want to work or execute projects and files and tweak systems setups on the host machine.

**Keylogger**

Otherwise called a keystroke logger, keyloggers can follow the continuous activities on their PC. It tracks every keystroke made by the client on using the keyboard. Keylogger is likewise an exceptionally significant threat to obtaining individuals' login details, such as username and password.

## Why is Computer Security Important?

In this advanced time, everyone wants to have their computers and personal details well protected, and thus computer security is imperative to keep our data ensured. Keep up with your computer's safety and general well-being by forestalling viruses and malware that affect your system's performance.

# Chapter 10: How to Protect Private Computer Against Installing Virus, Bugs, Unwanted Programs, and Hardware

Threats surrounding the security of personal computers are turning out to be persistently inventive nowadays. Computer hackers are attempting to get to your PC, worms trying to damage your computer, Trojans masked as pretty helpful programs, and spyware that obtain information on your activities and relate it to their owners. There is a need to gather all the required information and assets to shield against these intricate and developing PC security threats and stay safe on the web.

Some preventive methods to apply include:

**Get Anti-Virus Software Installed**

There are a lot of incredible packages of anti-virus software on the lookout. They help check and detect viruses by occasionally carrying out a scan on your computer. The vast majority of them likewise check for viruses on emails received.

Anti-virus software recognizes these viruses as indicated by its signature file. On recognition, it then takes good moves to deal with the corrupted files dependent on your inclination.

## Apply Software Updates Consistently

Another important advance to take is to ensure you have the most recent versions of all installed software being used. It is crucial because the regular software update adds features intended to withstand the most recent security threat. Microsoft, Oracle, and different producers consistently update their software to deal with "bugs" that hackers could take advantage of.

## Use Strong Passwords and Change Password Routinely

A primary password can be broken in a flash, while an intricate one might take longer to be discovered. Changing passwords consistently will make it difficult for somebody to access your computer using your password without you knowing quickly. All Windows accounts should attain a certain level of modification to have a secure password.

## Turn on a Desktop Firewall whenever Possible

A firewall is seen as a piece of hardware and software that makes a defensive hindrance between your PC and conceivably unsafe content or materials on the internet. It assists you with guarding your PC against hackers and numerous viruses and worms which attack computers. You are advised to install a firewall and turn it on before accessing the network.

## Be careful with Email Phishing Scams

Email is imperative to everyday life. Nonetheless, it is additionally the best channel to spread viruses and trap indiscreet users. There are various points to draw in clients to open malicious attachments or click links enclosed. Try not to open suspicious attachments or click on any suspicious links held in messages.

They can show up in Emails, tweets, posts, online advertisements, messages, or attachments, and once in a while, camouflage themselves as known and confided in sources.

## Backup your Files Intermittently

The internet has gotten fiercer, and techniques for attacks would never be depleted. It is possible to follow the preventive measures and have your computer hard disk failure due to ordinary mileage, making your information incapable of being recovered. In this manner, it is essential to back up your documents intermittently to get them retrieved when needed. The minimum you can do is back up vital files by copying or transferring such files into a flash drive or external hard drive.

## Install a Pop-up Blocker

Attacks on your computer can be through browsing the internet or web pages, which is your day-by-day online daily schedule. Hackers can access your PC by clicking an ad or link that is malicious. An advertisement or pop-up blocker is fundamental to ensuring your PC's information. It will keep any undesirable pages from opening consequently.

## Browse the Web Securely

Try not to visit sites that offer conceivably illicit and illegal content. Many of these websites contain malware or offer downloads that contain malware. Make use of an advanced browser like Microsoft Edge, which can assist with impeding pernicious sites and keep malicious code from running on your PC.

**Avoid Pirated Materials**

Abstain from streaming or downloading films, music, books, or applications that don't come from sources with good trust. They may be engraved with malware.

# Chapter 11: How to Setup a Remote Connection to your Computer

Remote desktop connection alludes to the innovation of accessing a distant computer without actually being there. An interface in software is provided between you and the other targeted computer. Access is created with the goal that the connection can be set up.

Microsoft's Remote Desktop Connection tool will allow you to get to everything from a remote place. With the computer being turned on and set up for distant connection, you can perform tasks, get a file or application opened, troubleshoot or simply work in a remote manner.

Through this desktop connection, you can, in a remote way, get access to different PCs over a similar network, regardless of whether they are somewhere else in the home or at the workplace

**How Does Remote Access Function?**

Windows Remote Desktop works by first distinguishing the device you need to connect. Then, at that point, your device needs authorization to establish a connection with the remote device. After the validation cycle is finished, gain entry into the resources of the remote device.

Remote Desktop Connection is incorporated into Windows and exists as a Windows 10 Universal application in the Microsoft Store.

**How to Set Up Microsoft Remote Desktop Connection**

To begin with, you or another person should sign into the PC you need to connect to remotely. The Remote Desktop on this computer is turned on by going to "Settings," clicking on "System," then "Remote Desktop." Turn on the switch close to "Enable Remote Desktop." Select "Confirm" to empower the setting.

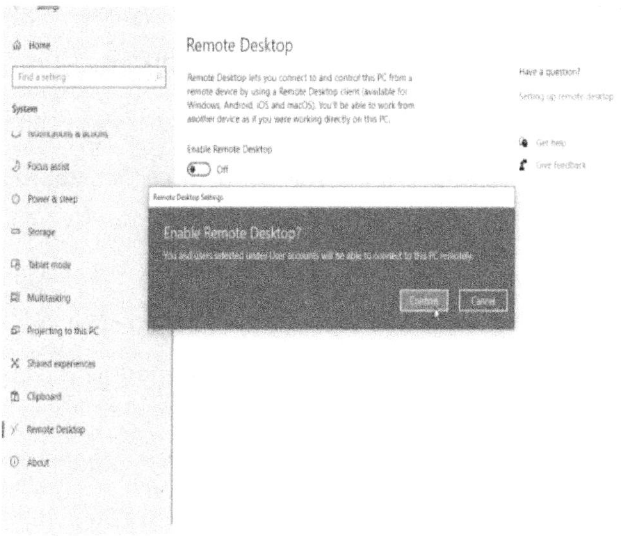

Remote Desktop can also be enabled using the "System Properties." Tap on the Windows key and input: "advanced system." Select "View advanced system settings."

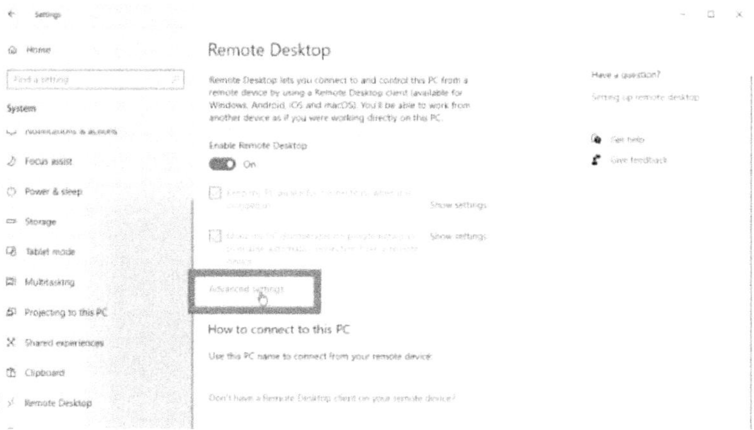

Select the "Remote" tab followed by "Allow remote connection to this computer." The box for "Network Level Authentication" should be checked. Ensure you enable incoming remote connections; the connection is established on the computer.

**Things to Note: Remote into Your PC**

How you want to connect remotely with the other computer depends on several decisions. You can use the custom desktop application or the Remote Desktop universal application. It's more flexible and can be used on platforms like iOS and Android.

For instances where there are many computers on the base network, a utility tool such as Advanced IP Scanner, which is unrestricted, can be used. Open the app and input a name for the computer or device. Add the IP address and click on "Connect." Then, enter the username and password you're establishing a connection with. Additionally, if you're going to establish a remote connection frequently, you can click the box to remember your details.

If you get a message indicating difficulty in identifying the status of the remote computer, click "Go ahead and Connect." To prevent another reminder, click the box. You have an idea of what you're doing.

There it is. Get on with the remote computer setup, remote support, or any way you need to utilize it.

**Using the Remote Desktop App for Windows 10**

As an option in contrast to the underlying Remote Desktop Connection tool, you can use the Microsoft Remote Desktop application in Windows 10. Get the app installed from the Microsoft Store and run it. The "Add" button is then selected, and then pick the option for a connection to be set up in Desktop.

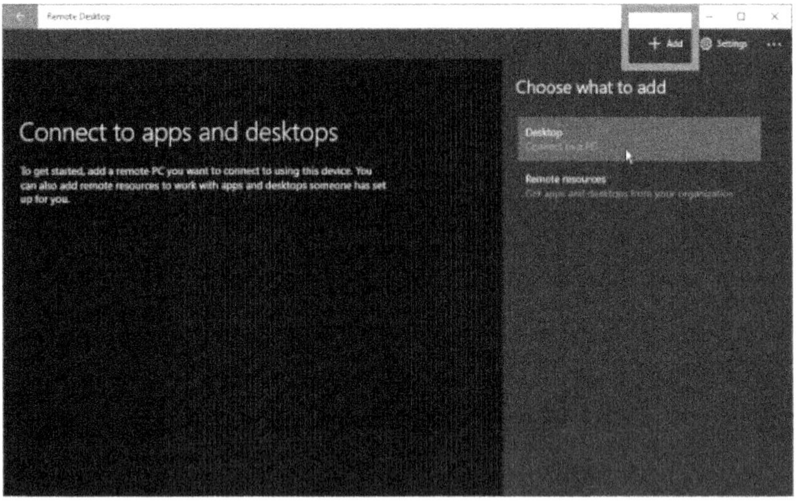

Put in the computer's name you want to connect with. You'll see a plus (+) button. Click on it to add the account. Input your username and password in the account window. If you want to add an account display name, go ahead. Select "Save."

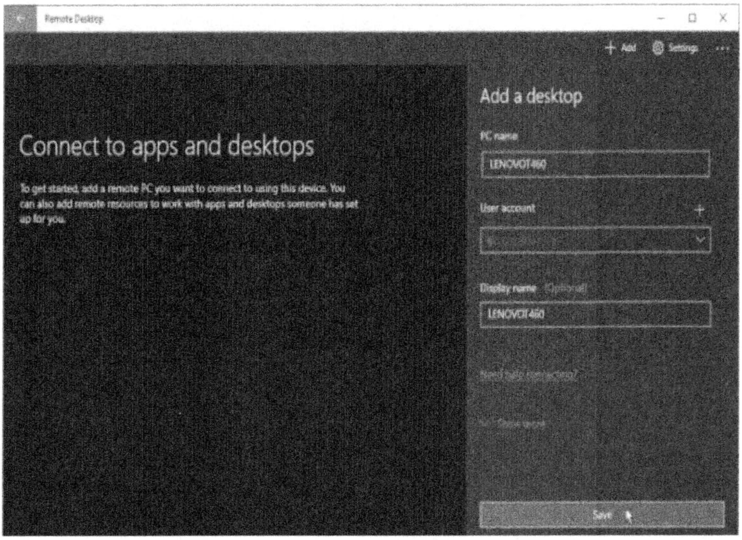

Double-tap the symbol for the remote PC to interface with it. At the authentication screen, click on the box close to "Don't ask about this certificate again." Select "Connect."

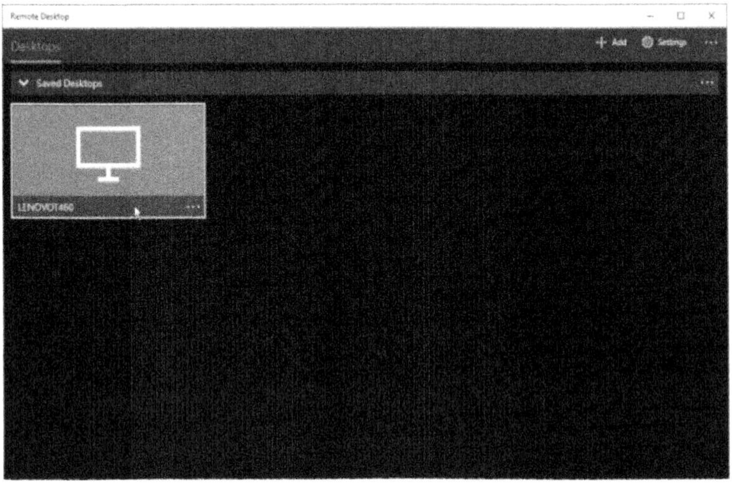

Connection is already established with the remote computer.

# Chapter 12: Backing Up Your Data (External Drive & OneDrive)

For a plan of retrieval or recovery of data, backup in full ought to be at the first spot on your list since it is the best technique against hardware failure and difficulty in-app upgrade and attack from malware that can ruin your files wreck your Windows 10. If you are not proactively making complete backups, you're putting your programs, files, media works at significant risk, and also setups

If you use Windows 10, you have a wide range of strategies to make a backup. For instance, you can use third-party applications or mediums to provide backup for the whole system or transfer files to an external drive, done manually. Backups can also be created by uploading files to cloud storage servers like of OneDrive.

### External Hard Drives

One of the most straightforward approaches to back up your documents or files is to duplicate them to an external hard drive. If you don't have one, buy one to get started.

### Backing up Files Manually

To back up some important files, create a copy of them and transfer them directly to an external hard drive, input the external hard drive into the port on the system, then click the ideal file and drag along to the drive. A duplicate is now backed on both the external drive and your computer

**Backing up Files Automatically**

To backup, first, fix your external drive into the required port of your computer, and then tap the "Start" button. Go to "Settings." Select "Update and Security." You'll see a rundown of options located on the left side of the Window. Select "Backup."

Click on "Add a drive" and choose the drive you just connected to your PC afterward. Assuming you need to stop there, you can. Windows will automatically create a folder on the drive and back up the files.

**Backing Up Your Files Online Using OneDrive**

Get your essential files, such as folders for your documents, Desktop, and pictures backed up with OneDrive folder backup. Doing so gets them secured and accessible on different devices.

If you see a prompt to back up your files, click on the prompt to activate the backup wizard.

If no prompt shows up, or you previously shut the wizard, click the icon in the form of a white or blue cloud. It can be seen in the notification area on Windows. Proceed to click on "Help & Settings," then "Settings." Click on "Backup" followed by "Manage backup."

The "Back up your folders" dialog ensures that backed-up folders are selected.

Click on "Start backup."

Your computer will start the syncing process to OneDrive. If you wish to close the dislodge box, go ahead.

**How to Restore Your Windows 10 to its Previous State (Factory Setting)**

Suppose your PC isn't functioning optimally the way it is supposed to, showing errors that are pretty strange or having slow performance. In that case, it's likely an ideal opportunity for a reset.

You may likewise need to reset your Windows 10 PC if you're trying to upgrade to an entirely new device and need to sell off the old one. Carrying out factory settings or reformatting your computer to a previous state can clear out any troublesome programs in the background and wipe unnecessary files off your computer's hard drive.

**Steps to reset your Windows 10 PC**

- Go to "Settings." Open "Start menu" and select the gear icon, the "Settings" option.

- Click "Update and Security"

- Go to "Recovery," seen in the left pane, and select.

- Windows gives you three main alternatives: Reset this PC; Go back to a previous version of Windows 10, and Advanced startup. Reset this PC is the ideal alternative for starting all over.

- Under "Reset this PC," click "Get started."

- You can now select "Keep my files" or "Remove everything," contingent upon whether you need to keep your information files unscathed. If that's not what is intended, the option "Remove everything" will perform what is spelled out, erasing the entirety of your files, photographs, projects, and other programs. In any case, the whole of your settings will get back to their defaults, and applications will get uninstalled.

- Despite your decision above, the following stage is to conclude whether to get Windows installed through the cloud or done locally from your device.

- Proceed to the next step. Click on "Next" if there's a prompt or warning from Windows that you will not have the option to move back to the previous version of the OS.

- Select "Reset" from the prompt. Windows will get to restart and take some time to get itself restarted.

Printed in Great Britain
by Amazon

27172767R10056